Landscape
with Plywood
Silhouettes

New Issues Poetry & Prose

Editor	William Olsen
Guest Editor	Nancy Eimers
Managing Editor	Kimberly Kolbe
Layout Editor	McKenzie Lynn Tozan
Assistant Editor	Traci Brimhall
Editorial Intern	Dustin Brown

New Issues Poetry & Prose
The College of Arts and Sciences
Western Michigan University
Kalamazoo, MI 49008

First Edition, 2014.

ISBN-13   978-1-936970-26-1 (paperbound)

Library of Congress Cataloging-in-Publication Data:
McCadden, Kerrin.
Landscape with Plywood Silhouettes/Kerrin McCadden
Library of Congress Control Number   2013949844

Art Director	Nicholas Kuder
Designer	Leslie Russell
Production Manager	Paul Sizer
	The Design Center, Frostic School of Art
	College of Fine Arts
	Western Michigan University
Printing	McNaughton & Gunn, Inc.

Landscape with Plywood Silhouettes

Kerrin McCadden

New Issues Press

WESTERN MICHIGAN UNIVERSITY

For my family

Contents

III.

IV.

Acknowledgments

Sincere thanks to the editors of the following journals in which these poems first appeared:

American Poetry Review: "Becca" and "Saint Athanasios at Meteora."
Failbetter: "The Domino's Pizza Gorilla" and "The Death of the Reader."
Green Mountains Review: "What I Said to the Night," "Bone China" and "Second Cut."
Hunger Mountain: "Definition."
Painted Bride Quarterly: "Say Sing."
PANK: "Safety Instructions," "Mostly, She Practices Falling," "How To Miss a Man," "Saint Albans" and "At the Pennsylvania Grand Canyon."
Poet Lore: "Ballooning."
Rattle: "Elegy for Some Beach Houses" and "Intersection."
The Salon: "Love Poem Not for a Husband" and "Bedtime."

"Becca" also appeared in *Best American Poetry 2012*, edited by Mark Doty and David Lehman.

Gratitude:

To The Vermont Studio Center for time and resources to work on these poems. To the many generous teachers at The Bread Loaf Writers' Conference, The Frost Place and The Colrain Poetry Manuscript Conference. To the good people at The Grind. To Montpelier Public Schools for indelible support, both material and personal.

To this clutch of writers, their good eyes and hearts: Ben Aleshire, Penelope Cray, Rachel Daley, Karin Gottshall, Major Jackson, Alison D. Moncrief Bromage, Alison Prine and Eliot Sloan. To Paige Ackerson-Kiely, Robert Barasch, John Bate, Adrian Blevins, Joshua Bodwell, Eavan Boland, Mark Doty, Gabriel Fried, Matthew Lippman, Fred Marchant, Alan Shapiro, Becca Starr, Karla Van Vliet, Ellen Bryant Voigt and David Wright for guidance and friendship in this art. To Lorrie Smith and Will Marquess for the bedrock; to mentors and colleagues at The MFA Program for Writers at Warren Wilson College for what comes now and next. To Rodney Jones for helping this collection find its feet. To Nancy Eimers, Kimberly Kolbe, McKenzie Tozan and everyone at New Issues Poetry & Prose. To David St. John, endless thanks for saying yes.

To my parents for unshakeable support. To Emma and Cal for our life along the Winooski River. To James and the Coy family for being family. To Cliff, for everything—from Siberia to spoons. To my colleagues, students, friends and family. I am so grateful.

I.

Becca

She says, *It's my birthday. I'm going tomorrow.*
What's your favorite font? What should I
have him write? Serifs, I say, *I like serifs.*
I like old typewriters—the keys little platters.
I don't answer the question about what to write.
The vellum of her back. I am not her mother,
who later weeps at the words written between
her shoulders. I get ready to retract the idea of serifs,
the pennants that pull the eye from one word
forward, but the eye loves a serif. When we
handwrite, we stop to add them to *I. Read this*
word like typeface, make me always published, I am
always a text. Write this on your back,
I want to say. Write that you are a lyric
and flying—serifed, syntactical. Becca chooses
Make of my life a few wild stanzas. She lies
on the bed while the artist marks her back,
his needle the harrow for her sentence. Make of
my life a place to stand, stopping-places, a series
of rooms, stances, *stare, stantia, stay.* She has
shown him a bird she wants perched above the final
word, *stanza.* It is a barn swallow—ink blue flash.
He says, toward the end, so she can know it will hurt
to ink so much blue, *I am filling in the stanza now,*
and he stings her right shoulder again and again,
filling the room of the bird. Make of my life
a poem, she asks me and him and her mother as
she walks away, make of my life something
wild, she says. I watch her strike out across
Number 10 Pond, the tattoo flashing with each stroke,
and there is barely enough time to read it.

Elegy for Some Beach Houses

The break off Chatham broke and spilled
old homes into the sea, just spilled them
like dresser drawers pulled out too far,
quiet underthings sent flailing like old aunts
into the surf. Just seaside, just at the beach,
just where the generations had combed for
jingle shells, whelks, the unrecognizable
bones of fish. Just there, the houses tumbled,
like only a house can, full of argument, debris
and leftovers. Just there, the houses groaned
like only a house can, full of mouseshit, must,
armoires and settees, full of lobster trap
coffee tables, old letters, tattered rugs. First the
buckle of underpinnings, then the hipbone
joists, the planks, the studs. The walls sighed
like pages wanting to turn, illustrated with
photos of old dogs, children, words
like *Beach, Happiness, Family* painted on shingles.
There was tipping and buckling and the keening
of nails pulling out. A roof wanted to slide, whole,
into the sea, but failed, the ridgepole splintering.
Its backbone broken and all the bits finished,
the houses were quiet. The old china floated
a bit, small boats. Newspapers, books drifted.
Daily trappings went down fast—some lamps, buckets,
deck chairs. This is not to mention all that sinks
right off (a watch, jewelry left on the sill). The fish
looked as curiously as fish can look, bumped cold noses
against dolls, mirrors, dishtowels like seaweed in the dusted light,
turned sideways, finned off. Little housed mollusks
made no notice. The ocean settled and
breathed, wave, wave, wave.

Mostly, She Practices Falling

And it is true that we are incredibly lonely.
That man walking the sidewalks of your town
with a tangle of bicycle innertubes
over his shoulder like a map of his heart,
running errands, studying a nest of bowls
in a shop window, which is also like a map
of his heart, may tell you he has given up on love.
It is the way he can go home and make rice
and sit with a book and not care that he is alone.
He says he has given up on love. He practices
saying this. What is true is that I have figured out
how to do it, how to live alone. I sponge off
the table, wash the plates, and go to bed.
Sometimes there is a dog. Sometimes
an extra blanket, which is a map as well,
folded and unfolded as needed, showing
the borders of one body within the state
lines of the bed. I am the marker—*you are here.*
The rest of the bed shows what we call
up north *the flats.* This is the topography of rest.
I am in my car, and the woman on the radio
talks about wanting to feel the most
intense physical sensation she can.
Instead of dancing, she practices falling.
She wants to make moves she can't help
but complete—mostly, she practices falling.
How far can she fall and not get hurt?
She wishes there were a way to measure
the intensity of pain. Before she dies, she wants
to feel it all. How far can a person fall onto a mat
and not die? This is the topography of grief.
Where is the edge of the heart, is what we want

to know. We are not afraid of words, we say.
All we can do is draw lines we cannot cross.
The words on the page are cursive,
the innertubes of thought we build into
what fine things we wish for, the trajectory
of our falling bodies, the edges of what we
can say, the things we say to the night.
Once, I held a bird in my hands. I held its wings
to its sides. Its feet dangled like the stems
of letters. There was no heft to it, just a cage
of bones. Just a cage of bones and feathers.
Just a house of air, craning its head toward
knowing something, staring into the middle
distance, suddenly calm. This is all I know.

Safety Instructions

Unless directed by a crew member,
do not construct if/then scenarios
—not about the plane, not about your life.
Unless directed by a crew member,
do not build flow charts for the past.
Do not sweeten your silence. Or the
beauty of the shoeshine man, who only
wanted your money. Do not consider
Denver in the rain. Unless directed
by a crew member, do not study the grid
of the western plains. The forked
and dissipating rivers do not translate.
They should not call to mind the footprints
of birds in the dust in your village. Unless
directed by a crew member, again, do not
study the western plains. Sometimes the fields
are crop circles, but these hold no mystery.
They are the elegant drawings, only, of rolling
gantries. When resting, do not lean on the man
next to you. Like the pilot, he will only talk to you
when you are making your descent into Chicago.
He will suddenly come alive, stop looking
out the window only to close the shade again quickly,
will ask his flutter of questions, then disappear.
Unless directed by a crew member, do not look
at the reading material of the men flanking you.
Do not show them the word they are searching for
is backward and diagonal. Do not reach over
and circle it. Unless directed by a crew member,
do not dream, in general, of men, or, in particular,

of one. You are suspended above the world,
a careening impossibility. You are flying, headlong.
As you fly East, the rivers are not isolated birdprints,
are a pulse. The forests return, dispatches from
the body. Unless directed by a crew member do not
calculate the weight of pronouns spoken by men.

The Death of the Reader

I have not read a book since my divorce, or,
I have been a bad reader and have read
books, but have not finished them, or, I may
or may not have read *some* books, but only
those I read as a child, and those to my son,
or, I have picked up books in order to love
them, but have been unable to. I have loved
so many books, and by that I mean novels,
those books that are to lose oneself inside,
to hide in a duck blind, to hide behind a door
with an axe, to hide in a tree with a friend,
to crush a birdnest in the fist to watch the
smallest shells fall through the sunlight,
to pick up a gun and fire it by accident
and kill my ten-year-old twin, my father
running through the tall grass like he is
under water, I have never seen him run
so fast. Even hiding in the farmhouse,
fantasizing about a floor that can be hosed
clean. Mostly, though, the duck blind,
and being caught there, my long dress
having trailed the mud, and later my death,
there, in the second-floor bed, my eyes
two awful things, my death a black thing.
This is the tenth poem I have written about
my death, or at least the death of the reader,
or at least the death of the reader who cannot
read books, only poems. A poem can break
your heart in the short term, and over and over,

in the same way, and in others, the shards falling
through the treelimbs to the pasture below.
This is the heartbreak I am after. Not the one
after the marriage, the long marriage, the forty
open acres of marriage, the fifty page ending.
Just the snapping open of a valve, the chamber
squeezing like a fist, my heart breaking like
a bird's egg, untended, desiccated, sparkling
in the evening light, so beautiful, so light
and diaphanous it almost doesn't fall.

How To Miss a Man

Breathing is just a rhythm. Tell yourself this so that the breathing
becomes a song. Sing this song all day while you shop in the hardware
store for things you do not need. Sing it again while you cook supper

for yourself. Cook supper for yourself, even if you don't want to.
Go for a walk, even if you don't want to. Put your shoes on
and get the leash and even bring the dog. She will be so pleased

you might start to forget. Also, breathe. It is a rhythm. Walk
around the block, and even farther, if you have a mind to.
You might. Your feet will take you. They can. If you listen,

they are a rhythm also. Like drums. Hand drums. Swing your hands
while you walk. Tell yourself they are kind of like wings,
that the bird's wing has a hand inside it. It does.

Come home and make tea. Every time you dip the teabag,
hold your breath like you are underwater. Hold. Breathe.
Hold. Breathe. Like that, like you are swimming across

Lake Pleiades, under water like a fish, above water like a bird
until you are stitching lake and sky. You are a needle just then,
darning holes in things, a weave of stitches across and down, like a graph.

You need to be a graph. A grid. Numbers are perfect. You can draw two
lines on a graph that can never touch. This is what you are building.

Ways To Say Goodbye

Drive through Wisconsin, where the antique shops
are closed. Closed-closed, the doors locked, the shelves
full of bakelite and ironstone and stoneware.
Also tractors and old trucks on the roadsides,

everything *for sale* for decades. You will keep driving,
which is not the same as picking the locks. No one
would notice things gone missing. You could fill your
truck bed. There would be that inverse relationship

between mid-west inventory and your truck bed,
but there are worse things to invert. This is a way to say
goodbye, incrementally, each shop peppering your
driving tour of the lake region. When leaving the ocean,

take walks later and later at night, skirting
the streetlights, finding beach after beach marked
private and sit in the dark at the edge of the wash
until all you can hear is the waves hissing like *sotto*

voce fighting across the dining room table after
the children have gone to bed. Take the rocks and shells
and seaweed and even the garbage inside the sweep
of your arms home in a plastic pail. When leaving a lover,

in the front yard, his truck packed, his house cleared
of your things, stand in the track his motorcycle made
when he rode across the front yard after work. Stand
on your toes and hug his neck. When you kiss him,

swallow the taste of him low into your gut. Later, when you
lay out the souvenirs of how you loved him, the skeleton
key, the rusted ring of metal he found and put on your
index finger, the buffalo nickel, the earwig that wriggles

out of your unpacked bag months later, you measure
how long this winter will be. It's all a contract
you made with the world, where you visit, and leave,
and take real and imagined souvenirs. At midnight

each night, you send an email to yourself, and to ten
strangers, filing a report on your findings, and your
leavings, so that someone will know where you've been,
and how desperately, like a child, you love the world.

Definition

I once found a deer collapsed near a lake—sleek,
immaculate, & unmoving except for its antlers, which swarmed

with orange-&-black-speckled butterflies that obliterated
the velvet beneath. Whatever word explains this,
I don't want to know it yet.

—Matt Donovan

The thorax needs to reach 59 degrees for wing-muscle to take flight.
Angle the thorax toward the morning sun, fold and unfold wings, body at rest,
and wait. During migration, find branches and rest in company.

Obliterate what you land on. Fold and unfold wings. The hinge is perfect.
The ornament of wings is more than we can bear. *Fold:* a prayer, asking
for *open*—the hemming of pants on a child, the folding, *hold still, hold still,*

fingers at the hem, the child on a chair, pins held in the mouth,
words spilling out the lips' crease, itself a furrow, funnel, runnel. Words
there like run-off, storm water. When I read, I dog-ear pages, turn

up the bottom corner when there is a word I like, like *fold.* I don't use a pen.
When the book is over, I go back through and find the words
I know I must have liked, and put them on my dresser. I took *fold*

because it was an old word. It doesn't need anything from me. It sounds
like *earth. Fold* used to mean *earth,* I want to say. *ða wæs winter scacen,*
fæger foldan bearm. Snow folds back like a sheet, uncovers earth.

It is all collapse and rise. Look at a child at a book of dinosaurs, where each page
turns and by some miracle of origami, dinosaurs leap at him, the bookjacket
flapping like wings, where he holds and releases beasts,

or a man who holds and releases a smile so that what remains are crow's feet,
the folded markers of joy, which open in sadness like washboards on a back road
in spring, mud sagging into release and capture,

or the old woman who was trapped in her foldaway Murphy Bed
for thirteen hours, some joke of eponymous law—*the space-making alternative
for today's lifestyle*—some old humor like what governs the folding of maps.

If, like Dr. Urquart, I put a monarch butterfly in a bag and hide it on a branch,
it will be joined shortly by another. So much for pheromones, or simplicity.
There is some system of wing-beats that speaks, some shiver of color

only they can see, the shift of shadow in the hinge of wing-folding, the kiss
of definition on stilled antlers by a lake.
                                        These are the ways I am folded by you—
into the light crease the store clerk makes to keep a receipt open,

make it easier to sign, the pressure of her finger holding it still,
into a cootie catcher, numbers and fortunes in the folds, into a string of cranes,
a rack of highway maps, a stack of clean sheets, into your chest

on a quiet road.
                    There were shadows—either from high trees weltering
or the wings on your back. Either way, they are pages now. I fold them back
into the night, each sheet a lakeside. I hardly recognize myself.

Love Poem Not for a Husband

Some days I am a mouth on a fish swimming
and swallowing the stream of things in front of me.
That old man—he is in my way, and I fall in love.

He is a fat peach in the intersection, small head on top.
He is old nails and grime. His arms swing like a child's.
People give him simple answers, and I want to take him

home, like a child, and wash him. A brace of a man
comes roaring down the tracks and his whistle sings through
the village. His wheels flatten the pennies I have set out.

Under the whistle is his engine in my breast rattling
my ribs like a grouse taking wing in the forest. He runs
right through me, and I watch him go, crestfallen. I fall

in love over and over. It does not matter. I stop a woman
by the firehouse. We swap news and I bend over her stroller.
The baby reaches for me, and so I pick her up. She dissolves

into a cloud of commas, washes down my legs and I coo
apologies to her mother, who has always known, she says,
that her little girl was just a series of pauses, waiting.

I walk down the farm road. I will visit a character
in a novel I have just finished, walk away from my place
toward her white house on the hill to have tea,

avoid my husband. I am charmed by the sound

of my feet on the dirt road, by the sozzled bee
that flies around my head, by the red-winged blackbird

that warns me from fence posts, from telephone wires,
from weed trees.

II.

Saint Athanasios at Meteora

I am arguing with my neighbor, John,
about health care, again, on the sidewalk.
Really, we are not arguing, but anyone
would think so by the way we flap and shout.
He is a wizened man shuffling up the walk.
His dog is ahead of him and stops when he stops.

The dog has a rope on his neck, frayed
from dragging on the cement. We have done this
many times. I am home from work. John is home from
his walk. Again. He says my name like a stone wall,
heavy and hewn. It is a three pound hammer
between thoughts. He gave his son

the name of a Greek God, not the kind who frolics
in the surf to the delight of vacationing women,
but a real one, who has probably been on a coin
and has spent much time jogging about the minds
of schoolchildren. An impossible god. Here,
said John to his son, here is your name.

He looks through me and into me and flails
about the injustice of it all. Yes, I agree.
OK then, he says, and heads the diagonal way
across Main Street to his upstairs apartment.
Up there, he plays piano. He has trouble walking
and uses a stick. His hip will never quite work for him.

He is the monk, I often think, of this village,
the concert pianist who can make you cry
when he plays. Here, his playing said to me one night

on the radio, come here. Climb this step, now this one.
Come with me up the stairs. Forget the war I fought in,

forget the one you fought at home. Walk up with me.
After the eagle brought me up the first time, he said,
I hauled people these thousand feet in a basket.
I walk with a stick now and have carved steps for you.
Walk with me. Soon, we will be above it all.
You should see the view, he said.

Intersection

At the four-way stop I wave you on,
a kindness. You wave *no no, you go*. I wave, *go*.
We keep on. You insist. Me: *no you,*
please. A bird shifts, a sigh. The penned
horse tosses, pacing. I mouth *you go*.
There is a fleck on your windshield. I notice your hands.
Rain falls. Your hands cup the wheel
at ten o'clock and two, then float
past my knee and only sometimes land.
One hundred times on my back, they tame me.
Cars line up. Birds lift. I nod my head into your chest.
There is a trail of clothing. I walk to the
plank door of your room. This takes hours
and hours. This is a small cottage and there is sand
on the floor and nothing on the walls, crows calling,
dishes in the sink. Days go by. We are still making
our way to the bed. This is an inventory:
black telephone, board games, frayed chairs, coffee
table spotted with the old moons of drinks, curtains
pulled back on tiny hooks, single pane glass
windows like the ones I used to sneak out of at night, lifting
them as slow as this stepping, and when you talk
into my neck the words settle in the hammock
of my collarbone, puddle there and spill,
slide over my breasts and I am slowly covered,
and rinsed. I do not close my eyes. Nothing hurts.
The dust rises in swirls. Dogs bark. You turn
your windshield wipers on intermittent.
Your car rolls into the space I have built between us.
I am up to my belly in a northern lake, cold. I am afraid now.
When I get home, everyone will see.

Insomnia

I.

The skin is a purse seine. There is an old man at the back
of the neck. He ties equidistant sheet bends during his waking hours
so that at night he can dream at the helm, hips squared,
cut the swells and his boat in arcs, net sliding through the fathoms.
The knots pull tight around his catch and the sternum,
all fins and tails, but mostly eyes.

I.

When the body is sleeping, there is sift, shuttle, meter. Shift,
treadle, metronome. Lift, settle, measure.

I.

A lyle gun goes off. The man whose eye is always to the sea
waves his arms. His sweater catches salt and his hollering is spray.
The gun fits its heft to the base of the neck, launches the hawser
past the shoal to the foundering boat, and the rest of the night
he winches the vessel toward the dock of the shoulder.
By daylight, the catch is loose, one man is asleep
in his station, one on a cot in a shack, and the boat rocks
against the neck like a tree ticking shingles raw.

What I Said to the Night

I.

All night I have folded laundry
into stacks that stand for children
gone to a father's house. All night
I have uncapped beer bottles,

stuffed firewood into the old woodstove.
All night I have uncorked old bottled up things.
The worst has been the longing
for you, old man. When I left you

there, on the ice, I had no idea the pages
would not keep turning. On the back shelf
of my heart I found some old scotch.
The box had wholesome paintings

& the corners were stapled. The cardboard
was thick, & the scotch was a waiting thing.
It was so precious I could not open it.
I walked upstairs, downstairs. I made myself

busy with Christmas, with a nap. I made
overtures to the night. I stood on the back
deck & threw my palms up in the cold.
I stood there, while the dogs did their

business, & prayed to the village,
please, to give me something other than
the police car flashing across the river,
more than the lonely security lights

on the Town Clerk's Offices.
O, lonely offices of my own, my palms said,
give me something to touch. Give me back
my children. Give me a man.

II.

My mind is a bowl. The laundry is chugging along,
& everyone is somewhere else. There is light
in the wood stove, light on the Christmas tree,
& light in my ribcage flickering

on this night that is so cold the dogs shrink
to go out in it. They look back at me
with their questions. None of my answers
make sense. I tell them we all must go out in it—

we are little god copies, nosing onto the ice—
we are furnaces in the night, lonely & empty,
piling stacks of t-shirts on the dining room table,
burying our noses into them. We are all

this lonely, lonely thing. We are the waiting
wings of January fluttering in the next-door
neighbor's yard. We are the stack of plastic
lawn chairs waiting for the thaw. Bring me back

my people, I want to say to the sleeping village,
or give me some new ones. Bring me a family,
for the love of god. I will sit it down to dinner
& ask it about its day. I will tuck it in at night.

I will suck in my breath as I kiss its temple
long after it has fallen asleep. I will walk the
dark halls of this house & listen for the lonely
thing, & I will kiss it, too.

Landscape with Plywood Silhouettes

He leans against the trailer, head cocked down
under the shape of his cowboy hat, matte black,
like the woman across the lawn near a patch
of low growing annuals, both of them as black
as the northern sky, as the dog sleeping in the shade,
as the old car on blocks. This is their courtship,
which the people in the house have long forgotten.
She is under the apple tree, holding her hand up,
waving a kerchief. He looks at his boots,
in that way a man will when he is actually looking
at a woman, across the lawn. She waves her kerchief
in the way a woman will when a woman is waving
a kerchief. She might be hailing a neighbor, a child,
the mailman, calling *yoohoo*. He thinks about her,
over there, calling *yoohoo*. She calls elsewhere,
but hopes that what he does is watch her raise
her arm. She hopes he sees that she can flutter
in a way he cannot. If it were not all black inside
the outline of her, he might see her mind working.
He imagines he can, since filling in the blanks
is not unreasonable in their world. There is only
what they can imagine. Also, he dreams up
eyes for her that are green, and a dress that is
blue and purple, and hair that is red. He watches
her smile, puts lipstick on her lips, smirks, thinks
hot damn. He forgets to make her eyes look sidelong
at him, which is what they are doing, looking sidelong,

noticing his downcast eyes under the shadow of his brow,
his toe that has just kicked at the dirt only moments
before she looked. She fills in his knuckles, the heft of his
shoulders, the belt, the buttons, the dust on his boots.
Hey you, she says, *it's a cold day for July,* thinks, *Honey,
what you know good?*—which falls on deaf ears, like his
Darlin', where you been? Come on over and sit a spell,
which she cannot. They dream and dream, notwithstanding
the way the layers of plywood have gapped in the weather
over the years since they began trying to bridge the void
inside their outlines, which is all we are ever able to do.

Skeletons

When we were finished talking at two in the morning,
and we were finished turning the truck on and off, on and off
to keep warm, and you were finished talking about all the ways

sadness stuck to you, all the book titles you would write,
all the rocks you had kicked as you walked toward home,
I went home and dreamed we were two skeletons talking

at the table. Your flap jaw kept moving in that fetching way,
its hinge clicking in that way it will when a man ages some,
and I sat quietly on my open bowl hip joints, shifting back and forth

from one curve to the other, careful not to scratch the chair, listening
to your outpouring with my skull holes, listening to your confessions
with my echo chamber. I looked at you, my sockets

misting over mid-story. When my turn came to tell you
what I thought, you could hardly hear me over the rattling
of my bones, cartilage long since thinned. I said you should

leave her. I kept rattling, long into the night. When you stood
to leave my kitchen, I stood to tell you I was sorry for my words.
You smiled in the way you could not help, and so did I, all teeth

and jawbone. Your eyes were empty, finally, and so were mine,
which was so much easier than before the dream, in which
I hugged you goodbye and clicked my finger bones against

your spine knots, locked my ribcage into yours.

My Brother Sits for a Life Drawing Class

The sun is out, and high, and the day is early.
The windows in the studio are clean, and so the light
is white, white light. My brother shows up early

and walks the room, touching things. He is building
thoughts. How can the world be this beautiful?
He brushes over wooden manikins and stacks of palettes

and tins of brushes and knives. Everything is a relic.
There are paintings of landscapes he thinks he knows.
He removes his shoes and clothing and wraps a dropcloth

around his hips. This is quick cash. The students file in.
He sits on a platform. In many ways, this is an escape.
They ask him to choose a focal point, and so he spends

the next hour watching the clock. He has always watched
the clock and never understood it, and so he is an expert
in déjà vu. In this hour, he becomes many-dimensional.

He is drawn from all sides and the composite witness heats
his chest to a small fire. This he knows already from needles.
Everyone can see that he is beautiful. In the sketches,

he is: an icon, a collage of bones and syringes, a man like a
smoke tree, his edges smudged until they are white;
he is afraid, his cheeks are drawn, his eyes will follow you.

There is another half hour. The students make him

more spindled and lank and wiry until he is almost a machine.
Some break the machine to look more like him.

They draw hands all over him, which, in the language of easels
means love. The students are young. Over the years, the sketches
will become sturdier. They will become installations

and sculptures and paintings of all kinds. One will become
a mobile like a bird. Because I think he will die before me,
I collect all of them. I build a room for my brother

and paint it white. I build him pedestals and good lighting.
I move my best chair in so I can spend days with him.
I come to understand. I begin to think I, too, am an artifact.

I become alabaster. People cease to understand me.
There is not much to say about this life and so I stop
saying anything. My words would be alabaster, too.

The curator calls the exhibit FORGIVENESS, for lack of
a better word. One day, frescos appear on the walls—a thin wash
of ghosts spot the landscape with their hands held out.

Fable

My son asks me to watch a cartoon with him.
The child is fighting with the father over how
it felt when the father left him. He is telling

his father both that he forgives him and that
though his father left the children with their
grandmother, it was not enough. The father

says the child is his world, and that he thought
about them every day. The child cries. They
stand on the deck of a ship, and the wind

blows the father's hair like it is underwater,
his hair moving as slowly as currents, like
anemones. The camera backs up, though this

is a only a series of drawings, and the father's
cheeks are an outcropping. The father is the
earth. The child knows this.

Ballooning

Dawn was pink, cold. Husks
of balloons grew—long thin
handkerchiefs into airships.
I sent her into the sky like a question,
stood in the driveway, smiled
the pasted smile of the stricken,
waved. She was ten. I could almost see
the light of my teeth. I was sure
they flashed *fight—flight*.
A balloon does not know where
it is going, and we gave chase,
there it goes, there it goes,
turning onto roads that thinned away.
She climbed and fell with shots of flame
along the river, then climbed so high
she became unlikely,
a lofty fleck of finespun color
spotting the gauze of winter.
For a minute, I lost her there.
Later, I thumbed through pictures
shot from the basket
and watched the morning—a flip-book:
There I was, smaller and smaller
on the driveway. The fields, too,
grew smaller and smaller.
Her hand dangled against the landscape,
smoothing the snowpack as she flew.
And while the sun finished cracking the horizon,
she arched back over the basket
and hung her hair into the sky.

Elegy for the Woman Who Became a Chair

She had always been comfortable, that was true
—a comfort, maybe, is a better way to put it.
She had a Sunday morning smile. And a patience
that was like a hassock. Many admired her ability
to look out a window. Some will say this was
because of the river, but a preternatural ability
to sit and pay attention cannot fully be blamed
on a river. Who is to say she did not create the river
by looking? When she was young, she was a rogue,
and did not sit for long. She spent years perched
and ready to fly away and years flying.
Everything was to be devoured, mid-air.
During the week she took to sitting,
there were those who worried and looked,
in different ways than she was looking,
but she was resolute. The looking in of others
was documentary, and did not create anything.
It was, however, a new pastime, and the others
had trouble doing anything else, after a time.
They could no longer answer the question
What are you up to? since, now, the answer
was always the same. They crunched equations
and figured she was the thing she was now *times*
the thing she had been, such that *hours* x *looking*
= *still life*, and *consternation* ÷ *worry* = *beatification*.
Like the man whose face becomes a promontory
by searching, or a child who becomes a whirligig
from spinning, the woman grew inextricably installed
by the window as a chair. She was not a machine age
chair, not a molded plastic shape-of-a-body chair,
she was not a naugahyde recliner, though all of these would

have done. She grew wings and claw-and-ball feet. She was
covered first in canvas, but soon grew to be covered in
scenes of historic balloon launches, the farmers running
at demon balloons with pitchforks, but many came to love her
in her most pastoral declension, stealing apples and fishing,
in love with a dandy, streamside. Neighbor children
climbed all over her and loved the things she said.
She said *find things to do in the body of a fish.* She said
track the flight plan of the mayfly. She said *put gloves
on the limbs of the boxelders.* She said *find a hiding place
for my words.* And they did, and went on speaking in core samples.
They drew the river on chart paper of all kinds. They mapped
the fishroutes. They spoke to each other in birdcode. They folded
their charts and graphs under their arms and walked out
into the world, whistling tendrils and leaf fall.

III.

Winter

Here is a little world that is the start of winter.
It is not very wide, or full of horizons. There are

two logs by the stove, and the woodstove gloves
have been set one on the other. Outside, there is

seasoned wood just delivered. Mr. Dix came yesterday
with a cord and a half and told stories. He used to live here,

across the driveway. Just like the woman who used to
walk the village did, his aunt killed herself on the bridge

up the road—fifty years ago, he said. Off the concrete bridge
by the mill falls. But not in the middle of winter, like the woman

I saw, who placed her sneakers side by side, a sock in each,
and dove onto the ice. When we reached her, she was broken

like a bird underneath a window, specks of blood in the snow.
She was dead and smiling and someone had to walk out on the ice

to get her. The ambulance that collected her took forever.
The truck's dump bed settled back down. A crow lifted

from the box elder with a great flap. Mr. Dix rumpled my son's hair,
took off his work cap to show what can happen to a man's hair

and climbed into the truck cab, said a couple of times
that it was nice to meet us, to stay warm.

Jake

This is Jake. He is not sure what you want
and so he will offer you everything. He wants,
say his eyes, for you to love him. He wants, more
than that, for you to forgive him. Here, he says,
is a fish. He caught this fish for you today. It may
have looked like he was running away when he
shoved off this morning, the haze a low smudge
bumping the island—it may have looked like
foreboding, his oars slicing the foam—like malaise,
his fingers trailing the still water—like endurance,
his arms a pair of explosions—like envy, his forehead
resting on the gunwale. It may have looked so much
like running, him skimming the sea toward the thin
line of *not-right-now,* of *later,* of *please, don't.*
There is salt water, of course, everywhere,
he smells like it, which is a smell like longing.
This is what a man offers. His ocean is wide,
the framing islands treed with fingers—everything
reaching, *please. Here is the fish I caught this morning.*
How wide the horizon when his line sprung tight,
how wide his eyes right now, the fish between you,
his eyes the same color the same shiver like mica like starlight
like sand in sunlight. His eyes tide pools. His eyes begging
right now. The fish between you, his eyes like fishlight,
the oars still, the boat rocking, the islands two sentinels,
the fish in his hands a found thing, his hands ringed
in sunshine, his hands, his face, his eyes under the halo

of this day. There is a cleft in his chin that divides his smile
from his frown. There is a gold light all around him, in and out
from his fingers, the island trees, the fish, there is a gold light.
This is a Holy man, you might think; you might also think
you are The Beloved. There is a halo of you, there,
right around his head, a circle of you. He is the word
of God, a letter from his island to your shoreline.
Open your hands like he does, like morning.
This is a reading from the coast of Maine.

Bedtime

When I have put my son to bed
and I have read him the story
and rubbed his back, and told
him everything will be alright
and the thunder storm has come
and gone, and the basement has
flooded, and the alarm on the
fire station has gone off not once
but twice, and he has squatted at
the top of the stairs naked as the
day he was born and said he was
afraid, and I have gone back up
and poured the glass of water,
what am I to do about the girl
in the white dress, who has
come back again, for the second
night in a row, her dress just past
her knees, which is all he can see,
and her feet, just standing there
in the doorway.

Little Ghost Girl

Little ghost girls are sometimes trouble. It might be just like
having any child. I always thought that, until I had one,
well, both. I have both now. Because she was never mine,
when I lose her, I forget to take care of her. She drifts somewhere
around the house. She doesn't make noise. Who even knows what
she is doing half the time. I have learned to call her Effie. *Effie,*
we're home! is what I forget to say when I walk in the door.
And when I am cooking supper, I forget her plate, which,
because she doesn't eat, is not the worst thing. None of us
remembers to ask her about her day. I read to her at night, true,
but that is an accident. I read to my son, and she is there,
but we both forget I am also reading to her, and sometimes
I make mistakes and read from a book of ghost stories.
This doesn't frighten my son, because he forgets about Effie,
but it does sadden the little ghost girl. Sometimes I hear nothing,
and I know that she is there. But what am I to do with her,
when I can't see her? She is like my brother and sister, long buried,
then, just nowhere. When she chases the carpenter away
from fixing things, she is trouble. I get mad at her then,
but, really, she's a good girl. I don't think she was ever mine.
I know she likes doorways—oh, and windows! I should not
have left my little ghost girl behind while the windows
were being replaced. I should have left the old ones alone.
She will think crazy thoughts about loneliness and being forgotten
again. I have never been good enough to her, my mouse, the little girl
I could never hold. Now that I am away from her,
she is all I can see. The small hairs rise on my arms and neck.
Soon, she will make me think she was once mine.

Once, I Was Not Lonely

Once, I was not lonely. I did not worry about
whether I was loved. I was two and laughed
at old women, stole their canes. I was five
and begged the milk man for ice and kicked it
in the street. I was ten and accused everyone
of cheating at kickball, threw balls at other
children from a speeding bicycle. I was twelve,
thirteen and was still an island, an island that,
despite appearances, did not drift in the sound
with the tides. The houses were small, cedar
shingled, shuttered with green shutters.
Gulls sat on the rooflines. None of the houses
faced the others. This is the kind of island I was.
Boats came back and forth, mostly working boats,
weathered and painted with working names.
None said *For Sail* or *Knot Working.* The engines
blatted and the sails flapped. The waves were calm
and were not calm, they were breath. Once, I was
not lonely. I looked east and west, drew lines
north and south, watched while the sun drew
arcs through unanswerable skies.

Tom and Jerry

The cat is bonking a bird on the head with his fist,
while the mouse ties the cat's tail to a telephone pole
and, in a split second, saws the pole through and with
his mouse finger, topples the pole.

A cauldron is over a fire, the bird wears a hard
helmet. The cat is flung from a cocked sapling
into the cauldron, is scalded free of his hair,
and he finds himself suddenly embarrassed.

The bird and the mouse have ganged up on the cat,
who has spent most of his life in pursuit of the mouse,
whom he cannot have, because it is not in the cards.
The mouse will always win.

The cat dances on an electrical wire and is
electrocuted. He chases the bird with Wright
Brothers wings he has suddenly concocted and
falls to the ground. He will always lose.

Next, he lurches into the basement with a crate
marked DANGER (missiles and a launcher). The mouse
threads the cat's tail through the missile. The cat
launches it, unaware, and threads himself through a tree.

There is nothing to be done by the cat, now, but to string
Christmas lights along a runway for the bird that ends
in the cat's mouth. This will go well, will result in blue skies
and cartoon clouds, a jet soaring overhead, with its nose

in the cat's mouth. The cat is exhausted. The silent mouse and the bird who makes the sound of electricity whenever he moves have won. I am pretty sure they make that sound with a hand saw, I say. *What?* my son asks, startled.

Laika

How do you tell your children it was never easy.
That the boards you planed to build their house

were contracts. The nails you dropped were pleas.
How do you tell them the bushes you planted

to build the yard never got the boundaries right.
A flock of cedar waxwings drew better boundaries—

shaking the hedge so you couldn't look away,
no matter which chair you had fallen into, exhausted.

Instead, tell them about Laika, how no one expected
her to survive space orbit. That they sent her up anyway,

just to see. She went up and achieved weightlessness
before she died, a few hours into the flight. Tell them

about the cover-up, the story they told for decades
about her living six days in her rocket home, being a

dog-in-space, spinning gracefully in her ellipsoidal nest,
food and water nearby, held securely by her safety harness,

panting the dog smile that sometimes means panic, but looks
a little bit like happiness. I think I was weightless once.

Ante Up

This is what you said to me this morning, at the breakfast table,
but not really. What you asked me was *what would you give up*
and I have been thinking about that all day. I would give up,

for instance, the rocking chair, but not the dresser. I would give
up the rugs but not the table. I would give up the books, even,
but not the letters. I would give up the farm, but not the paths

worn into its fields. The sentences without semi-colons, but not
the lovers who wrote them. Well, it is true that I have given up
the lovers already, all of them, but not the plot chart of them.

I would give up all the lakesides, but not the late afternoons.
The dusk sky, even, but not the swallows. The front and back door,
but not the neighbors. The map, but not the way here.

Nevermind the fact that you never asked me this, that I read it in
the Book of Questions you brought in from the truck after the road trip.
We were road weary, and suddenly unsure. I have spent the day

in writing formulas and calculating risk. What I have come to so far is this.
I would not give up the sling of your mouth, the bit of silence you hang
between words, the interstitial gaps of your teeth, or your string of guesses

after I ask *guess what?* I would not give up the machinery of your gait,
not even for a nightly return to the beginning.

Saint Albans

We made love, algebraic and steady.
Soon, you left for work. I spent the day
like foreign currency, ambling. I was an
angler fish. You were bioluminescent,
right past the bridge of my nose all day.
I followed, and also did not follow.
I bumped into things all day. I went to
the library, where none of the books would
tell me about Pushkin, where the librarian
cut coupons and set a timer on my use
of the table. The logs in the fireplace
had never been lit. I went upstairs to
find the rest of the books, and found,
instead, offices. Everything was under
water, my apologies to the librarian
for the pile of books, the smell of my
leftover sandwich. I could not work
around you. When I left the library,
there was police tape to my left, and
I drove the wrong way down the street,
women with strollers milling on the
sidewalk, waiting for something to emerge
from the house between the library and
St Mary's Church. Everything was
under water, the skateboarders, the
rubbernecking women who had heard
this was a methamphetamine bust

in this sleepy northern city, this city
where the sidewalks are planted with
low flowers in geometric patterns, each
one a separate lure, the soil dry between
them, this city named after the town in
England, it turns out, where the Magna
Carta was born, the rights of the common
man, this city so asleep on the beach
it does not know how far underwater
I can breathe, or what I see, the way lit
as it is by a cold light. I am as alone
as I can be, just now, with the city
pressing in, the disapproving woman
who almost hits me as I drive away
shaking her head, but I am increasingly
alphanumeric, making more and more
sense the closer I am to home.

The Domino's Pizza Gorilla

Have you seen our gorilla? Late one night,
she was stolen—the plate glass shattered
and nothing else taken. Not the cash register,
not the pizza boxes, not the scenes of Sicily.
Have you seen our gorilla? Cars go by for weeks
and no one brings her back. Joe won her at the fair,
slammed the hammer hard enough to bring her home,
googly-eyed and lumpy in the way of all cheap imitations.
She sat in the corner under the fern. The first time
you held my hand, she was right there, our gorilla,
watching in that weird way gorillas watch us,
like they know what we are thinking. *Have you
seen our gorilla?* I'm pretty sure I have, says
the woman who goes in one day, says she saw her
up at the Granby Zoo. There was an extra one
last weekend, she says, in the gorilla house.
The silverback lolled on his back and scratched
his crotch like a man so pleased he doesn't care.
It was awkward, this story she told, and they assured
her their gorilla was not alive. Oh, she said, confused
about their concern. *Have you seen our gorilla?* does
not mean the gorilla walked away, is somewhere
afraid in the cow fields of Vermont, cold, hungry.
It means she is sitting next to the bong in someone's
apartment, chatting with the boys who stole her,
watching them wide-eyed and unblinking while
they tell her secrets. *Have you seen our gorilla?* is

the question the sign asks for weeks until we almost
believe we have lost something like a child.
People walk in all month like seekers of the Loch
Ness Monster—photos of her everywhere, shadows
on buildings, *I think that's her!* This town comes
alive to find her. The answer to the question becomes
a resounding *yes*. Everyone has seen our gorilla,
everywhere. *Have you seen our gorilla?* She is quiet
and sits in corners. She is a shadow and a watcher.
She is a witness. She saw you hold my hand, she saw
those boys make mistakes they will not remember,
she heard us in the night. She airbrushes shadows
on buildings—things shaped like fear and lurking
and pining and love. We have been up all night
looking. First we combed the fields on foot, calling
the soft noises she makes when she is sad, which are
kind of like the low growl of the diesel truck
we back out of the garage to trawl the backroads.
The engine calls to her like a lover. We call to her
in low sounds we almost remember, startled because
the heavy maple branches squeaking against each other
are like the sound her stuffing makes when she walks,
this bigfoot dreamwalker we laugh to find ourselves out after,
two beers in the console, Johnny Cash on the radio,
the two of us gone around the bend, as moonstruck as the fields,
hunting for something no one else can find.

At the Wellsboro/Johnston Airport

Yesterday we drove so far from home
even the grass was strange. All day I sat,
a frozen road warrior, past abandoned homes,
past the Lobster Shack/Hotel whose sign offered
Gurls, Wed Night, a landscape of eternal promise.
All day I wished I had taken a picture of that sign
and thought about just about everything as the lines
on the road droned like the airplane engine you were headed
to fix when it finally got going, the Johnstons watching
from their golf cart—the flying team from the fifties—
for whom the airport was named, these two
now calling each other *mother* and *father,*
watching you prime the radial engine until it makes
its low growl, so low it is almost only a thumping
inside our ribs, your trick of coaxing an engine
to life—the engine that, once in the air,
though it may pump and thud like a heart,
the small plane actually does not need
to bring itself safely to the ground.
This is what I tell myself weeks later
when I hear that Mr. Johnston has died,
that his wife sits on the concrete porch
by herself in the evenings, swatting flies.

At the Pennsylvania Grand Canyon

After taking a series of self portraits
with a 1930's incinerator, which was
covered with lichen and spiders and rust,
a series of close-ups of the coin operated
view-finder—*step up* and *turn*
to clear vision, I took a series of portraits
of myself with the bronze 1930's CCC Worker,
who was looking off into the middle distance,
wherever that is, and looking a little
long suffering. I sidled up, and in much
the same manner that I take all my shots
of myself—trying to catch myself
unawares, mid-expression—I tried to
catch myself and the statue in a moment
of intimacy. I snaked my arm around
his neck, my hand casual against his
collarbone, and looked off. We looked
together into the middle distance, into the air
bowl of sky that is the canyon's yawn. Then,
I leaned toward him, so that my head rested
on his shoulder. Then, I nuzzled in, for real,
there, on the constructed walkway,
mid-trail, at the edge of the canyon, even my dog
looking askance at us. I stood there until
the people stopped staring, until the weather
burnished my skin that same sun-brown, until
my dog walked away with the young girl
who had asked so nicely, so much earlier,
to pet him, until all I could think was how

I wanted to look into his eyes forever, despite
his pupils being awkwardly cast, like two
small finger prints, as if someone once tried
to reach inside them, how I wanted to brush
his cheek with the backs of my fingers
in the dark, where no one can see me cry
and some twist of metal in my chest
is tightening and I can feel it shiver,
how I would never be able to, turned to
bronze like this, stuck out in the various
weather, him caught mid-kiss with the top
of my head, stuck there like that, how I
would stand like this forever, caught in the act
of desire, frozen before reaching or speaking,
how I got, in the end, what I had always been after.

IV.

Nostalgia

There is no market for sincerity, I say, walking away
from today's parade, which marched twice around
the village green. We work from booth to booth

downing lemonade, being propositioned
by the scout leader organizing a rubber duck race, by a man
hawking strawberry shortcake. His shirt is as crazy

an American flag as the one the next town over
hanging like a lolling tongue thirty feet up
off a hook and ladder. *Strawberry shortcake?*

he says, holding up his tray. *You'll be able to do
anything you want after you eat it.* Leans closer.
You can fuck all night long. Swings up his voice

at the end of *long* like a songbird. We raise
our eyebrows to toast his offer. He looks like he wants
to join us. It is the hottest day of the summer,

almost so hot his offer doesn't sound like
a good deal. We walk away, past a brick house
gardened in front like last night's fireworks.

In the center of the yard is a plant that is more
constructed than alive, seems built of rivets
and rust and faded aluminum rocketing into

branches over and over until it is so tall we have to

open the back gate and ask what it is. The old woman
tells us she grew it so people would stop by and ask

what it is. *Take some,* she says. *Here is where
the young plants are. Come back when it is not so hot
and we'll dig you some.*
                              What were you saying

about sincerity? he says. *Follow me,* he says,
and we skirt around the back of the town garage
to run our hands over a mid-century tour bus,

fallen to rust. We touch the turn signals, yellow
on one side, red on the other, the rivets, the windshield
wipers, which have not rusted. *When people rode*

this bus, I say, *men wore fedoras because that's what
men wore.* I look through the window holes and see
their shadows. He says, *I would love*

to restore this, walks past the International
plow truck, same vintage, plow rusted solid to it,
says it cannot be done.

Bone China

I raise a glass at a friend's house. Everyone
toasts their day, and I toast this day that is
not a day. I raise a glass. I always wanted
a long marriage. When we built a home,
the foundation was too high, and the house
became a ship. You know how ships are.
I found myself always on the bow. There is
little to say, beyond that. I was on the bow.
The waves were a giant hayfield. I watched the stars.
I wondered what a sextant was. I leaned my hips
against the porch rail during storms. Yes, of course,
my hair whipped in the wind and mist. Sometimes
I wore a dress. I was a tragic figure. I watched for
land. Today, though, we toast other things, not
my wedding anniversary, which no longer exists,
like the marriage. I wonder if everyone can see
the black hole of it, right next to me. We raise
glasses to our health, the weather, new jobs.
The back deck is old and weathered. The children
captain innertubes and capsize in the pool below.
We toast new tattoos, phone apps, things we should
get to some day, upcoming trips, the late June sky.
Let's raise our glasses to this little beast next to me,
my little emptiness. See how it follows me around
today? I can't help wanting to offer it something.
The world says china. That is our gift. The best
china is made from bone. Mix the bones of cows
with clay and feldspar. My friends keep going around
the circle, offering wishes and clinking pints, while

in some alternate universe, he and I—the man himself
and I—continue what we had abandoned. I hold
out my hands, which are full of bone, and he holds
out his, and we grind them, those tools, down to
bone ash, then slurry. Before long, we are tired,
like we always were, and nap under the black willow.
This is a kind of dance that happens in other worlds,
where what is on the inside is turned to the outside,
and little by little, we become ugly and strange. Our
bones become racks and the wind comes through them.
The music is old. When we wake up, we are tangled,
useless, our bones confused and mixed in a heap. When
the rain kicks up, we are already translucent. Everything
has been ground to a powder and we can do nothing,
not one single thing. The bones of cattle are greater than
we are. In the end I am a platter. I lose track of what
he becomes, but I know that if you flick our edges
with your thumb, we ring like bells. I always wanted
a long marriage, grown children organizing surprise
parties every ten years, tins of casseroles lined up on
tiny sternos. When I set out my dinner plates later,
way up north, and the manure trucks amble by late
into the summer day, I hold each plate up to the light
to see my hand through it. The Indian paintbrush
is blooming. I am just in from a walk, and the mallow
reminds me of those years. I rang a bell in a high white
church one day. The cows were lowing in the heat.
The whole world seemed translucent, and I a fine
white powder, blowing away.

Commute

On the way to work this morning, there were goats
in the road, a herd of them, like an island of small
uncertain deer, confused by the pavement beneath
them, but also exalted by their breakthrough
so that the ones at the fringe hopped with their
heads tilted like teenagers gone mad with their
music. It was as lovely a thing as a sunset
on the drive home, come over a ridge and
the low sky is a settlement of orange, dense
and hot against the treeline. There were women
with umbrellas and milling men. For a long time
we all sat there, commuters and farm trucks
and goat farmers and this large scatter of goats,
dead center in the road, for long enough that
I gained a sense of place. Soon, the border collie
was down the farm road and biting them back
into their field to blend, like most days,
into the burdock and milkweed. Little by little,
we all drove on, the scene becoming, while dodging
potholes, a key to something, a wind-up toy to set
loose. My answer to the Rorschach test is the collie.
My answer to your questions about what is wrong
with me, the goats' eyes flashing—a cross between
Morse and binary codes. I keep these answers to myself.
I will never write back. Little by little, we all drove on,
the morning just as gray and muted as any in October
before the leaves light the hills and we sit back
in our chairs to re-read warmth in translation
and other illegible texts.

Dear Day in Late September

I am not sure how you will receive this, but I am sure of my
need for momentum and a kind of seasonal loneliness,
which I blame on you, thus this letter. Anyway, on my mind
are the increase of dark and the rows of vegetables
out back that have become an embarrassment of weeds.
While you are a day in late September, and a day with high
humidity and raindrops sitting and not drying or freezing
on almost everything, you are also a day with a morning
like early June, but with a thinner sun. You are a day
with dahlias and dahlias and geraniums, and myrtle
underfoot. You were a morning fat with bees and you
are all day long a river. There is not much else, but I think
I am coming to know you. Earlier, I wanted to call you a liar.
My windows are open, and the air is lovely and I fear this
is a cruel trick. My jackets stand ready. In any case (forgive
my impertinence!), I ask for the usual, freedom, still,
from sadness. And since there is an increase of darkness,
and also this great momentum, I want to tell you I am
thinking about closing up shop for the winter. I am settling
my accounts. Enclosed, please find a brace of birds,
which I hope you will accept as payment against last winter's
oil bills. There is much to do. Up in the barn, I have spelled
out the name of the man I love with crabapples. It is one way
to know a man's heart. I believe in his name, though,
like I believe in good gloves. Oh, how we fight the cold
with everything we have. There are more words here for cold
than for snow. *Is it cold enough for you?* we ask, but words
freeze so quickly when it is two clapboards below zero, September.

Sometimes it is so cold we just say, *Christ!* The weather is coming.
The ducks just flew north up the river—just now. I will go now.
I am not sure how many animals I can feed through the winter,
and there is reckoning to be done. My ledger says things
I am afraid to share, even with you. I work on closing up
the house. My empty windows should be filled with poems
against winter before the day is through.

UVB-76

There is a dog barking on a leash strung
between the building and a tree. The trees
are pine, and the branches are low.
It's a ring of trees, and the dog barking,
he barks like a ring of noise. If you wait
for him to stop, you will wait.
It's what happens when you wait,
an impending sense that nothing will ever happen.
Here, it is true. And none of the mothers
and grandmothers and children
of the men who are gone will tell you
anything you want to know, except this
was once paradise. Inside the stone structure
is a dark hole that is deep enough to lose time in.
When you toss in a rock, it is easy to lose track
of how long it has been falling. The noise
of the bottom being hit should come sooner,
shouldn't it? Nothing should be so deep,
especially the gap between two people.
Sometimes, when I listened to him talking,
his anger became a kind of tapping music,
steady, like rain falling on the roof.
And far away, like he was an action figure
of himself. They were not words he said,
they could not have been words.
I saw him forming them with his mouth,
but once he launched them, I didn't know
where his words went. They went on and on

but I couldn't decode them. They were
tapping and ringing and buzzing, yes,
buzzing in short, sharp blasts, like at the tower
beyond the stone house, where an open
microphone sits in front of something
that somehow calls its mechanized birdcall
every other second without fail from its red
and white rusting Cold War era tower,
only broken three times in decades, so that
those who love it listen to the buzzing
on their short-wave radios in hope
and fear that it will stop, like the way
some nights I listen to my heart beating,
so regularly, and before long, I am listening
for it to stop, and am horrified that it might,
because, well, it will, and so my life is
also a waiting for things to stop.
For so long I waited for things to stop.
And they did not make sense, his words
that sounded like insects on a hot night,
like cicadas on full volume and sped up
until they were buzzing like something
hot and electrical that you wouldn't
want to touch. I would turn my ear to them,
turning knobs on consoles until I thought
I knew what he was saying, until the signal
from his brain into the air between us became
more like bells, and then I knew at least
what bells were. I found a decoder ring

in Voyenni Gorodok. When I turned it,
I heard whales, The French Resistance,
sometimes the Gongs of Saipan, sometimes
a signal sent up to measure the ionosphere,
how high is the ceiling of the sky.
These were words I could understand.
And when I broke the code,
he became so small he disappeared.
I fell in love with the world all over again
and fell asleep to its steady drone.
I wrote across the night sky. At the end,
I wrote *Love* in cursive and as a post-script,
said *Write back to me with every kind*
of regularity—because, really, I am in love
with regularity—the regularity
of every kind of thing. It is how I am
carried like a ticking bomb to my end,
pulsing, a wild hand playing piano like
a desperate wish. Remember, you are human,
I said to my ear that could no longer
understand speech. One night, I snuck
away and climbed the tower hand over
hand. This took something like years,
hand over hand. I climbed, and listened
to the chirping and humming of the
short-wave signal that was part heart
beat and part hardware hitting a flagpole
in the wind, part door-bell ringing over
and over, begging are you home? Can I
come in? I said, I'm coming.

Apology, Its Absence

I.

Here is the acre after the string of words and before
the reply. Here is the dirt road slung between them,
these two villages, pitted and beautiful, something

around each bend at which to exclaim, *look*. Mark
the longitude and latitude, the fields a blank morning
stare. Here is the snow the Holy Roman Emperor

stood on barefoot for three days. Here is the moment
before the Pope raised his chin to him to accept
what may or may not have been sincere, which has

little to do with forgiveness. Here is a sterile room,
and here, the moment after my mother daubed
her mother's lips with lemon and ice, the moment

just after she said with her hands what was not
to be said, which was *I'm sorry*. Here is that stretch
of quiet—the four hundred years it took the church

to apologize for locking Galileo up for life. Here is
the middle of the night when apologies were not made,
over and over, back to back, the breathing all wrong.

II.

Here are two lane roads. Here is the spot just before
we arrive, where we are sure of where we are on a curved
surface, where we are not sorry, but locked into contour.

Here is a carved picture frame, and its smaller velvet mat,
and its smaller subject, a wax cast of Pushkin's stomach,
cast by a witness just as mesmerized by the two

perfectly mirrored circles: belly button and bullet hole.
Here are these landmarks, calling to each other, one inches
above the other, this geography stunned and framed

in a small museum I visited with you, last summer,
off the interstate in New Hampshire. I was lost
in that landscape, between two coordinates, one as round

and perfect as the other, its revision, no apologies
to be made, each O a silence, a north and a south.
I could not find my way out, or the way back.

The Southern Tablelands

There is a town here called Worrowing,
which I spend the day considering as a verb.
I conjugate it in various ways as I drive
through the Southern Tablelands—*how
I am worrowed* is the one I say over and over.
The smaller the road here, the more parrots
I startle. This track is one lane, the eucalyptus
overhang, and the parrots, red and green, fly
through the funnel of trees. When they have
resettled, I can't find them. My heart curls up
to rest, and I flush cockatoos. What does it mean
when birds like owls back home show the way?
I turn onto smaller tracks, where mailboxes have
rusted bullet holes and a shit-stained lamb hobbles
down the track. It will not come to me and I am
no one to walk into the grass in this country,
my ankles bare. Here is Wollondilly Creek. When it
floods, check the meter markers. They climb to 4.
Decide whether to cross based on this. Today
the water is low, but there is grass on top of the
stockade fence. The musk duck is a piece of night
on still water. I float away slowly. The warnings
here are charms—wombats, kangaroos ahead.
I have watched the roadsides from Goulburn to Nerriga.
Here is where I find them, Nerriga's dusty road.
There is a boxy utility shed for something—telephone
or electric. There is a rundown outpost. I get out
of the car, get back in. I fumble with the camera,

then can't bear to look through a lens. I want to be
like them, resting squat on my haunches, rooted almost
to the earth. I am always full of their leaping, and my
hands are small, and always held out. All day I have
held in them the words you said this morning before
I drove away, your arm across my shoulders, my
morning bare feet unsteady. You and I grow old.
Our ears are full of ringing, and, now, of the calls
of birds—songs I strain to hear and know. The galah
is as beautiful a bird as I have known, clustered
on the road to the bush airport, having chosen one house
to haunt. Every day I drive there to see them,
colored like clouds and blood. This is a terrible way
to end a poem, but you and I have been at this game
so long that *I love you* is a secret as unexpected as
roadside parrots. When I open my mouth to respond,
they are what fly out.

Second Cut

I want to put this nectarine and these hayfields into this poem,
the valley filled with chainsaw music, treelimbs objecting,
the saw singing like a throaty bird. I want to put in last night's red
sun that the camera couldn't catch—no matter how many times
I tried, it just looked like the moon. It is a little box, a poem,
a thing full of blackbirds bolting from the maple, hermit thrushes,
always in pairs, first one, then the second, that hawk sailing over
it all, this day so hot, it's like a painting. In paintings of haying,
the masters often chose the colors of maps—peaches and blues
and soft greens. As if the world were a guide to itself, the hayrick
a country, the bales, the haywagon, even the men, the beasts—
all governed spaces, places to spend time, regions, all of them,
discovered and charted, the painter saying *here, this is the way
here,* so that your heart had a place to land. Out back here,
the farmer races the weather, leaves the second cut of hay to dry,
the whole field a clockwise spiral. Day and night, there is a
tangle of men in the valley, not the white-shirted, rope-belted
men from the paintings—shirtless men on tractors, four wheelers,
in pickup trucks, on haywagons, wiry and filed, sweet like second
cut hay. The word *hay* means *hewn, cut. Heawan.* Second cut,
like the ridgeline on the way home, where above one ridge,
there is another, darker, the same shape, saying *first, second.*
This old word for hay looks so much like *heaven* I am confused.
First, there was someone—a husband, second, there was you.
The second cut is always sweeter, something these old farm hands
will tell you sure as shit over a beer, or by the gas pumps
at Stone's, the vowel sounds they make growling like engines,
their eyes warm as the late sun I couldn't catch.

Say Sing

This is my one life. Say you know.
Say this means many things, say snowy owl,
say three feet of snow, say kestrel. My one
life is here at the table, next to me. Say you know,
say fine night for soup, glad to have you,
how was your drive. Say there is only one ridgeline
worth knowing, one swale between three hills.

Wonder why the mountains are named
Lord's Hill, Devil's Hill and Burnt Mountain.
Say we should go there sometimes, when we are lonely
like this, stand in the center, gear shouldered and
wonder where to camp. Say bear claws and hawk
circles, say grass chewed low. Say here,
One Life, settle in with us. Here is the fire.
Say here is a warm stone. Say sing.

Notes:

"Becca": *"Make of my life a few wild stanzas"* is a misappropriation of a line from "A Dream of Trees" by Mary Oliver. This poem is for Becca Starr.

"How To Miss a Man": "Breathing's just a rhythm" is from the song "One More Time with Feeling," by Regina Spektor.

"Definition": The epigraph is from Matt Donovan's poem, "Fumbling with a Field Guide on the Back Arroyo Trail." *"ða wæs winter scacen, fæger foldan bearm"* is from *Beowulf.* Translated: "Then winter was gone, fair was the Earth's breast."

"Saint Athanasios at Meteora": Meaning "suspended in air" in Greek, Meteora is a group of monasteries in central Greece, each built on a column of rock rising over 1300 feet into the air.

"Elegy for the Woman Who Became a Chair": This poem owes "find things to do in the body of a fish" to Dan Albergotti's poem title, "Things to Do in the Belly of a Whale."

"Jake": Alison Goodwin's painting by the same title is the basis for this poem.

"Dear Day in Late September": Michaelmas, the feast of Saint Michael the Archangel, was a medieval English holiday celebrated to mark the end of the harvest and the coming of the winter dark.

"UVB-76": UVB-76 is a mysterious shortwave radio station that broadcasts a short buzz tone 24 hours a day. The buzz tone is broken very infrequently by voices speaking in Russian. Although it has somewhat of a cult following among shortwave radio operators, its purpose is not known.

"Apology, Its Absence": A wax cast of Alexander Pushkin's stomach, preserving his navel and its neighboring bullet hole, is on display at The Main Street Museum in White River Junction, Vermont, among other curiosities.

Kerrin McCadden's poems have appeared in *American Poetry Review, Rattle, Green Mountains Review, Failbetter* and other journals, as well as in *Best American Poetry* and The Academy of American Poets' *Poem-A-Day* series. She is the recipient of a National Endowment for the Arts Literature Fellowship, support from the Vermont Arts Endowment Fund and The Vermont Studio Center. Currently a degree candidate at The MFA Program for Writers at Warren Wilson College, she also teaches English and Creative Writing at Montpelier High School. She lives in nearby Plainfield, Vermont.

The New Issues Poetry Prize

Kerrin McCadden, *Landscape with Plywood Silhouettes*
2013 Judge: David St. John

Marni Ludgwig, *Pinwheel*
2012 Judge: Jean Valentine

Andrew Allport, *the body | of space | in the shape of the human*
2011 Judge: David Wojahn

Jeff Hoffman, *Journal of American Foreign Policy*
2010 Judge: Linda Gregerson

Judy Halebsky, *Sky=Empty*
2009 Judge: Marvin Bell

Justin Marks, *A Million in Prizes*
2008 Judge: Carl Phillips

Sandra Beasley, *Theories of Falling*
2007 Judge: Marie Howe

Jason Bredle, *Standing in Line for the Beast*
2006 Judge: Barbara Hamby

Katie Peterson, *This One Tree*
2005 Judge: William Olsen

Kevin Boyle, *A Home for Wayward Girls*
2004 Judge: Rodney Jones

Matthew Thorburn, *Subject to Change*
2003 Judge: Brenda Hillman

Paul Guest, *The Resurrection of the Body and the Ruin of the World*
2002 Judge: Campbell McGrath

Sarah Mangold, *Household Mechanics*
2001 Judge: C.D. Wright

Elizabeth Powell, *The Republic of Self*
2000 Judge: C.K. Williams

Joy Manesiotis, *They Sing to Her Bones*
1999 Judge: Marianne Boruch

Malena Mörling, *Ocean Avenue*
1998 Judge: Philip Levine

Marsha de la O, *Black Hope*
1997 Judge: Chase Twichell